The First-Timer's Guide to Origami

By Jill Smolinski
Illustrated by Neal Yamamoto

LOWELL HOUSE JUVENILE

LOS ANGELES

NTC/Contemporary Publishing Group

To Daniel Smolinski Elder,
the best origami airplane maker I know
—J.S.

Published by Lowell House
A division of NTC/Contemporary Publishing Group, Inc.
4255 West Touhy Avenue, Lincolnwood (Chicago), Illinois 60712 U.S.A.

Managing Director and Publisher: Jack Artenstein
Director of Publishing Services: Rena Copperman
Editorial Director: Brenda Pope-Ostrow
Project Editor: Cindy Chang
Designer: Carolyn Wendt
Cover Photo: Ann Bogart
Cover Models: Marisa Jackels and Jamie Fredrickson

Lowell House books can be purchased at special discounts
when ordered in bulk for premiums and special sales.
Contact Customer Service at the address above,
or call 1-800-323-4900.

Printed and bound in the United States of America

Library of Congress Catalog Card Number: 99-76525

ISBN: 0-7373-0370-0

RCP 10 9 8 7 6 5 4 3 2 1

Contents

About Origami

How can a penguin look like a flower? Or a boat like a bunny? When you're folding origami crafts, they're all the same at one stage—before you begin! Each origami craft starts as a simple square of paper. Then, by folding it in a certain way, you can change that square paper into something entirely new.

Origami is a Japanese word meaning "to fold (*oru*) paper (*kami*)." It's been around for more than a thousand years. Children in Japan learn origami when they are very young—often before they learn to read or write. Now origami is a favorite pastime among American kids too.

For first-timers, origami can seem like a mystery. This book was made just for beginners like you. It shows you everything you'll need to know to get started making origami crafts, even if you've never folded anything before—even your laundry! So get ready to have fun, and get folding!

IT ALL BEGINS WITH A SQUARE PIECE OF PAPER

When folding the origami crafts in this book, any thin, square paper will do. Special origami paper that is white on one side and colored on the other side is available at art-supply and other specialty stores. Origami paper can be fun to use because sometimes both sides of the paper show in your crafts, so it's like having two pieces of paper in one. Wrapping paper also works well, or you can even try newspaper for making really big projects. Unless it's required, avoid construction paper. Even though it comes in great colors, it's very thick, which makes it frustrating to fold.

HOW TO MAKE A SQUARE FROM A RECTANGLE

Most of the paper you have handy is probably in a rectangular shape. It's easy to cut it square so you can use it for your origami crafts. To do so:

➤ Set up your paper so it looks like the illustration shown here.

➤ Fold the right top point over so the top edge lies flat against the left edge.

➤ Got it? Now use your fingertips to flatten the fold along the right side of your form.

➤ Cut off the bottom strip. When you open your paper, you'll have a square.

GETTING STARTED

In this book, you'll find step-by-step instructions for completing lots of crafts. Each one is made up of folds simple enough for a first-timer like you. When learning anything new, however, it takes time to get the hang of things. When you first picked up a baseball bat, it probably took a few swings before you hit the ball. You'll find the same is true when you're folding origami. It will take practice to get it perfect. That's okay! In origami, the fun is in the folding. You're sure to have a great time while you learn!

THE BASICS

Here are some things it helps to know before you start.

1. Gather up your supplies before you start folding. Often, all you'll need is a square piece of paper. Some of the crafts require scissors or things for decorating your finished pieces.

2. Always do your folding on a smooth, hard surface, like a table or desk.

3. Follow the directions shown for the craft. Don't skip any steps.

4. Take your time. Make sure all folds are as straight as possible before you move from one step to the next.

5. Don't focus just on the finished product. Enjoy yourself along the way! Give yourself a pat on the back when you try a new type of fold, or if you figure out a step that may have seemed hard at first.

WORDS TO KNOW

You'll find these terms used often throughout this book.

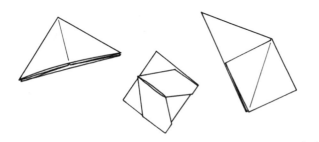

Form

The craft you're making is also called your "form." So if the instructions tell you to turn your form over, it means the piece of paper that you're folding.

Point

A point is just that: a pointed edge on your form. Sometimes your form will have three points, and other times it will have many more.

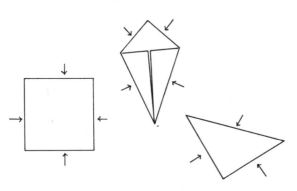

Side or Edge

A side or edge is any flat edge of your origami craft, either on the left, right, top, or bottom.

Crease

A crease is the edge or line that you get when you make a fold. It's shown in the illustrations as a thin line.

 ① 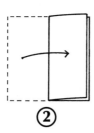 ② 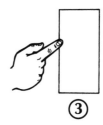 ③ 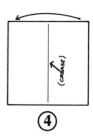 ④

You've folded a piece of paper in half before, right? You made a crease when you ran your fingers down along the edge to flatten it. See? You're already on your way to being an origami expert!

HOW TO FOLD

In origami, there are several basic folds you will use again and again.

Valley Fold
Fold the paper toward you.

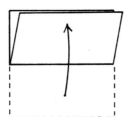

Mountain Fold
Fold the paper away from you.

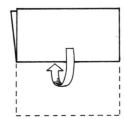

Squash Fold

This fold is usually called for when two sides of the flap need to be squashed flat. To accomplish this, poke your finger inside the flap and—you guessed it—squash it.

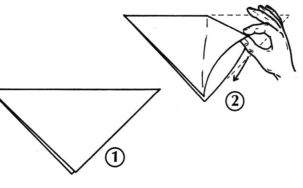
① ② ③

Folding a Point to a Point
Carefully line up the two points, one on top of the other, then crease any folds.

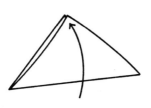

Folding a Point to a Side
Fold a point over so it touches the very edge of a side.

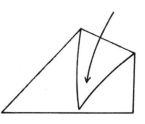

Folding a Side to a Side

Lay two sides against each other, make sure they line up, then crease any folds.

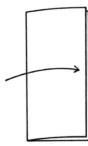

Turning Your Form Over

Pick up your form and turn it over so the side that was facing up is now facing down.

Turning Your Form Upside Down

Unlike turning your form over, turning your form upside down means to rotate it so the top becomes the bottom.

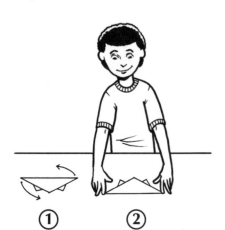

① ②

BASIC FORMS

Many origami crafts begin with one of many basic forms. Here you'll learn the forms that are the foundation for some of the origami projects in this book.

BASIC FORM 1

1. Begin with a square piece of paper in a flat diamond shape, colored side down. Fold your paper in half, bringing the left point to meet the right point. Then unfold to see the crease you just made.

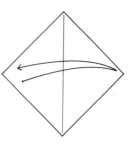

2. Fold the left and right sides to the center crease so your paper looks like a kite.

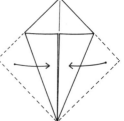

BASIC FORM 2

1. To make this form, begin with a square, colored side down. Fold your paper in half, side to side, then fold the top edge down to align with the bottom edge. Now open it up to the original square and fold it diagonally both ways. Reopen it.

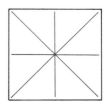

2. Fold the paper in half to make a rectangle. Then fold it in half again to make a small square. Lay the square flat on your table with the open ends facing down and to the right.

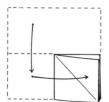

3. Now hold the top flap straight up and poke your finger inside until it reaches the very tip. Carefully squash the flap down to form a triangle. You should still be able to see part of the square from the other side. Be sure all your corners line up and look pointed. Now turn the form over and repeat this step on the other side.

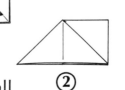

BASIC FORM 3

1. To make this form, you must first follow Step 1 in Basic Form 2.

2. Lay out the origami square in front of you in a diamond shape, colored side down. Fold the paper in half, bringing the top point to meet the bottom point.

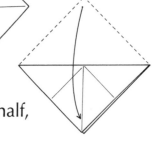

3. Carefully hold the right side of the form open at point A, then squash-fold it by pushing down on it to meet point B. Does it look like illustration number 2 on the right?

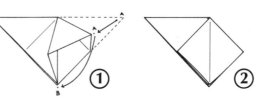

4. Turn your form over and repeat Step 3.

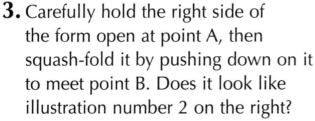

The Straight & Arrow

It doesn't take a bow to send this arrow soaring—just a piece of paper and a steady aim.

MATERIALS

- origami paper

WHAT TO DO

1. Start with your origami paper in a square, colored side down. Fold the paper in half by bringing the bottom edge to meet the top edge, then unfold it.

2. Fold the top left point so it touches the center crease. Repeat this step using the bottom left point.

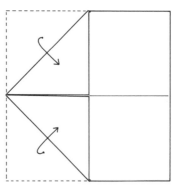

3. Do you see the diagonal edges that meet in a point on the left side of your form? Start with the top diagonal edge and fold it so it lies flat against the center crease. Repeat this step with the bottom diagonal edge. Make sure that the point on the left side of your form stays nice and pointy!

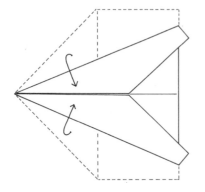

4. Now fold the top edge of your form to meet the center crease. Repeat this step with the bottom edge.

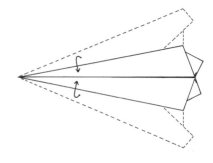

10

5. Turn your form over. Fold the bottom edge up to meet the top edge, and crease sharply.

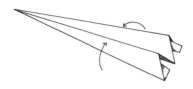

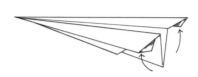

6. The flaps on the front and back sides of your form are the arrow's "wings." Lift each wing up, and your arrow is ready to hit its target.

SOME STIFF COMPETITION

Do you prefer an arrow that flies straight and fast? Or do you like to watch it float freely? The paper you choose can make a difference. Stiff, heavy paper makes an arrow built for speed. The lighter the paper, the slower the ride. Test for yourself. Fold arrows using various types of paper. Stand in one spot, then give each arrow a send-off.

FiRST-TiMER'S TiP!

YOUR WORK SPACE
The best place to fold your origami crafts is on a hard, flat surface, like a table or a desk. It lets you line up your folds without everything getting all wobbly. If you try folding forms on your lap or—even worse— while holding them in your hands, you'll find it harder to make straight folds.

Big Birthday Crown

It'll be a birthday fit for a king or queen when you make this crown for a friend, family member, or even yourself!

MATERIALS

- 20-inch piece of square paper (for a kid-sized head)
- glue
- glitter
- sequins
- number stencils
- pencil
- scissors

WHAT TO DO

1. Begin with your paper flat in a diamond shape. Fold it in half by bringing the top point to meet the bottom, and make a sharp crease.

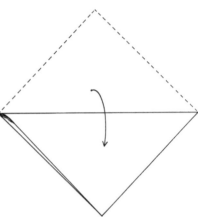

2. Fold the left and right points to the bottom point.

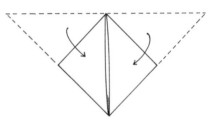

3. Look closely at the illustration for this step. Remember the points you just folded to the bottom? Starting with the left point, fold it back up and at an angle, creasing it about an inch below the top edge. Repeat this step with the right bottom point.

4. Now fold the bottom point (front flap only) up to meet the top point. Make sure you get it all the way up so the two points line up at the top, then crease it well.

5. Use a mountain fold to fold the remaining bottom point up to meet the top point.

6. Trace the birthday boy's or girl's age on a piece of paper using your stencil. Cut it out and glue it on the front of the crown. Decorate with sequins and glitter, and place it proudly on the lucky wearer's head.

TEENIE QUEENIE

Turn your stuffed animal collection into a royal court by folding up miniature crowns. Follow the directions above using a 6-inch square of gold or silver metallic paper. Write the animal's name on the front of the crown along with its royal title, such as "King Bear."

FiRST-TiMER'S TiP!

BE KING OF THE MOUNTAIN FOLD

If the instructions call for you to use a mountain fold (such as in Step 5), that means to fold the point or edge back, away from you. This can be tricky since you can't always see where you're going! To make it easier, peek to the back as you fold to make sure you're lining everything up right. It's also okay to turn your form around so you can see better—just remember to turn it back again before moving on to the next step.

Frame It Up

Do you have a lot of favorite photos just lying around? Put them on display in this paper frame you can make in minutes.

MATERIALS

- 8-inch square of origami paper

WHAT TO DO

1. Begin with your paper in a square, colored side up. Fold the paper in half from side to side, then top to bottom, to form creases that run up and down and across. Reopen it into a square.

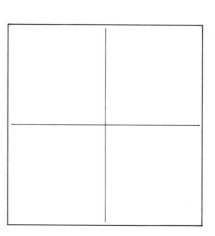

2. Fold each corner point to the center of the form.

3. Turn your form over. Then fold each corner point to the center again.

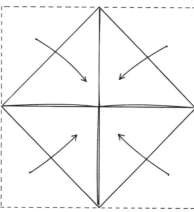

4. Turn the form over again. You'll see that it now has four square flaps with points that meet in the center. Use a valley fold to fold each inside point to its outside corner. Run your finger along the fold to make a firm crease at the base of each of the little triangles. The front of your frame is complete!

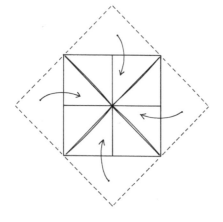

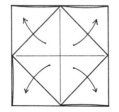

5. Your frame will be able to stand on its own if you just reach back and unfold the triangle-shaped flaps on the left and right sides so they stand straight out. Set your frame down to see how it rests on the bottom edges of these flaps.

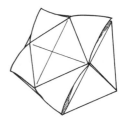

SMILE & SAY BEEEEADS!

Glue beads or other decorations on the frame's front corners. Then find a photo that's about 3½ inches square. Slide the photo into the frame so each of the photo's corners rests underneath a corner flap. Use a larger piece of paper to make bigger frames for bigger photos. Just remember your photo has to be square to fit into this frame.

FIRST-TIMER'S TIP!

MAKING A SHARP CREASE
Want to get your creases super sharp? Right after you run your fingertips along the edge of a fold, go over it again with your thumbnail.

Springtime Bouquet

Can't wait for spring? Fold up a garden full of tulips that will add sunshine to your day any time of year.

MATERIALS

- 4-inch square of origami paper for each tulip
- Popsicle sticks
- green watercolor paint
- paintbrush
- glue
- scissors
- green paper

WHAT TO DO

1. Begin with your paper flat in a diamond shape, colored side down. Then fold it in half by bringing the top point down to meet the bottom point.

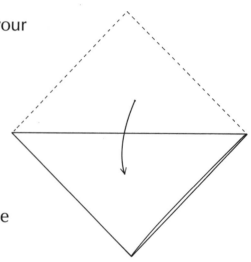

2. Fold the form in half again by bringing the left point to meet the right point. Crease it, then unfold.

3. Now fold the left top point down so that the top edge is at a slight angle from the center crease. Repeat this step using the top right point.

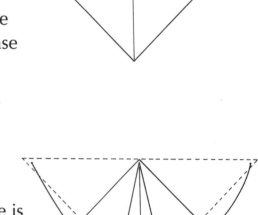

4. Use a mountain fold to fold the left and right points back. Turn the form upside down, and there's your tulip.

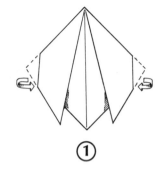

① ②

5. To make a stem, start by painting a Popsicle stick green with watercolor paint. When the paint is dry, glue on leaves cut from green paper, then glue your tulip to the top of the stick.

POTTED PAPER PLANTS

Want a great way to display your paper flowers? Pot 'em! An inexpensive clay pot will do. Just set a block of Styrofoam inside, then poke the flower's stems into the Styrofoam. Cover it with a layer of dirt, and set the pot by your window or in any spot that could use some springtime cheer.

DID YOU KNOW?

The valley fold, which you do when you fold a point or edge forward, is the most common origami fold. It's hard to imagine making an origami craft without using at least one valley fold!

Tumbling Toy

When you give this tumbling toy a nudge, it'll do a complete somersault. It's so much fun to watch, you'll give it a perfect "10"!

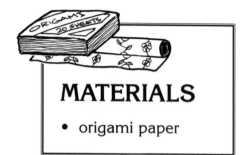

MATERIALS

• origami paper

WHAT TO DO

1. Start with your origami paper in a square, colored side down. Fold the paper in half by bringing the bottom edge to meet the top edge, then unfold it. Fold the form in half, left to right, then unfold it.

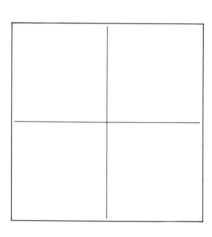

2. Fold the bottom edge up to meet the center line.

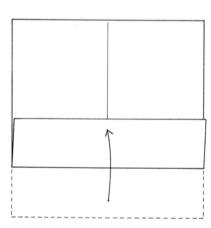

3. Use a valley fold to fold the left and right corners to the center line.

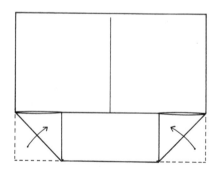

4. Fold the bottom edge to meet the center line.

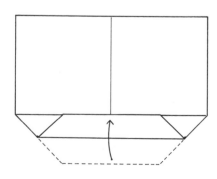

5. Carefully fold the left and right sides to the center line, and crease them sharply. You may find it hard to get a straight line at first because the bottom of your form is so thick, so take your time! Then unfold it.

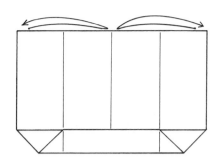

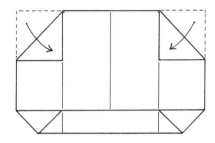

6. Fold the top right and left corners to the creases you just made.

7. Fold the left and right sides again to the center line (like you did in Step 5). This time, rather than unfolding them, let them lift up so the sides are at a right angle to your form. Your toy is ready to roll.

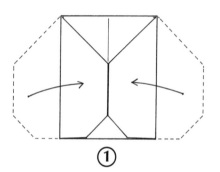
①

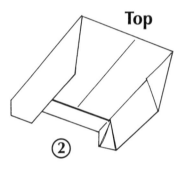
Top
②

8. Set your tumbling toy on a table or other hard surface. Tip the top of it forward, then watch as it rolls the rest of the way on its own.

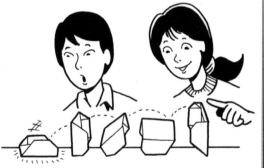

WHY DOES IT WORK ?

The side of your form where you made the most folds is heavier than the other side. When you tip the toy, the heavy part drops to the ground (as heavy things will), and the force of motion is enough to bring it around full circle.

DID YOU KNOW?

When you play with your tumbling toy, you're joining in on a tradition that's hundreds of years old. Children in Japan learn how to make fun things from paper starting at a very young age. Hey, who needs to go to a toy store when you have a piece of paper?

Whale with a Tail

Do you think you need a boat and binoculars to spot a whale? All you really need is a square piece of paper to have a whale of a time.

MATERIALS

- 6-inch square of gray origami paper
- scissors
- markers

WHAT TO DO

1. Begin with Basic Form 1. Turn the form around so it looks like the illustration.

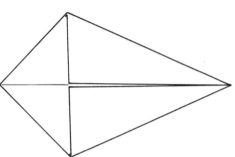

2. Do you see that when you folded the two sides of the "kite" together, they formed a vertical crease? Fold the left point over so it just touches that crease.

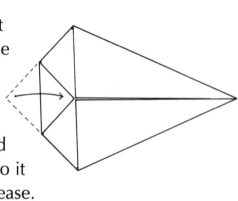

3. Now fold the top point over, creasing it about a half inch from the top. Repeat this step using the bottom point.

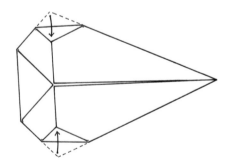

4. Your whale will take shape when you fold the form in half by bringing the bottom edge to meet the top.

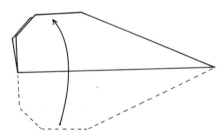

5. Use a mountain fold to fold the whale's tail back. Crease it sharply to hold it in place.

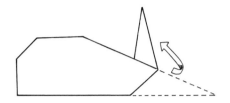

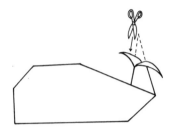

6. Ready to make a whale of a tail? With your scissors, cut a line down the center of the tail about an inch from the tip. Separate the two sides by folding one side at an angle from the other side.

7. Use a marker to draw in the eyes and a big smile. Then congratulate yourself for doing a whale of a job!

SPOUTING OFF

When a whale comes up to the ocean's surface, it sprays water from its blowhole so it can breathe air. You can make a spout that's just right for a paper whale. Cut three lengths of curling ribbon, and tape them to the top of your form—and thar' she blows!

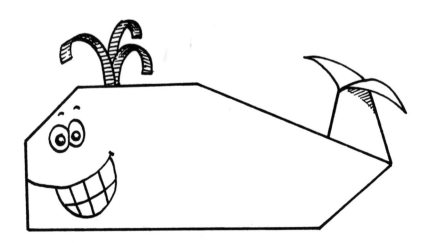

WHY DOES IT WORK ?

When making an origami craft, you sometimes have to make a fold, only to then unfold it! First-timers often think this is a waste of time, but it's not. Undoing a fold makes a crease. You need creases all the time in origami. Try to notice how often you're instructed to fold a point or side to a crease, and you'll understand how unfolding in origami can be just as important as folding.

Party Popper

You'll be amazed at what a big noise this little piece of paper can make.

MATERIALS

- origami paper

WHAT TO DO

1. Begin with your paper in a square, colored side down. Fold the form in half by bringing the left side to meet the right. Then unfold it.

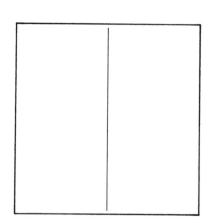

2. Fold the left side to meet the center line.

3. Now fold the top edge to meet the bottom. Crease it firmly and your popper is complete.

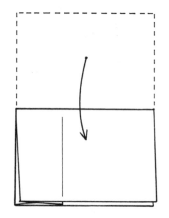

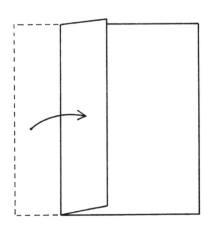

4. Ready to make some noise? Pinch the popper by its upper right corner. Then flick your wrist quickly downward through the air (the same motion you'd use for a yo-yo). The popper will open and, as it does, make a loud snapping sound.

22

HAPPY NEW YEAR!

Party poppers are a great New Year's Eve noisemaker. Try folding some up in bright colors to ring in the new year with a "bang."

FIRST-TIMER'S TIP!

TRY, TRY AGAIN

Sometimes you get partway through folding a form and—ugh!—you realize that you messed up along the way. This can be discouraging. It might help to keep in mind that the joy of origami is in the folding, not just in the finished product. Be proud of all the new skills you're learning, grab a new square of paper, and try, try again.

Cuddly Bunny

You won't believe how a basic triangle-shaped form is just two simple folds away from becoming a bunny. Sound too good to be true? Get some paper, and get hopping!

MATERIALS

- origami paper
- colored pencils
- cotton ball
- glue

WHAT TO DO

1. Begin with Basic Form 2. The open flaps should be facing upward to the right as shown.

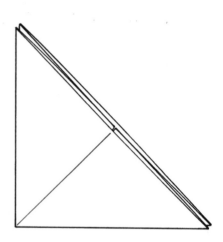

2. Use a valley fold to fold the top left corner (front flap only) over so it sticks out over the long edge. The crease should not begin at the bottom corner, but a little higher up as shown. This will be your bunny's ear.

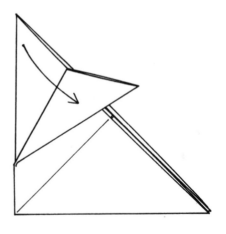

3. Turn the form over and repeat Step 2 on the other side. (This time, you'll be folding the top right corner over.)

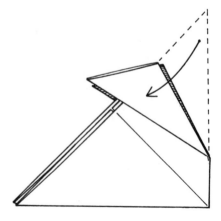

4. Set it down and you'll see that this rabbit can already stand on its own! Just use colored pencils to draw on eyes, back legs, and whiskers, and to color the inside of the ears pink. To add a fuzzy tail, glue a cotton ball in between the two outer sides.

THE BEST NEST

Here's a fast and fancy Easter decoration. Cover a paper plate with Easter grass, sprinkle it with jelly beans, then set your bunny in the middle.

FiRST-TiMER'S TiP!

USING A BASIC FORM

Why use basic forms? They're one of the few shortcuts you're allowed to use in origami! Once you learn a basic form, you'll find you can use the same steps to make many other crafts. The triangle-shaped form used to make the bunny, for example, is also the basis for the peace crane on page 74. Learn a basic form once, and use it again and again.

Bottoms-Up Cup

Grab a square of paper and make a cup that really works—but only once, and only if you drink fast!

MATERIALS

• origami paper

WHAT TO DO

1. Begin with your paper in a diamond shape, colored side down. Fold it in half by bringing the bottom point up to meet the top point.

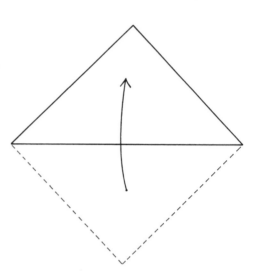

2. Fold the bottom left point over so it touches the right edge. Make sure that the top edge of the flap you're folding forms a straight line across your form like you see here. This will eventually be the rim of your cup. Is it a perfect line straight across? Then give it a good crease!

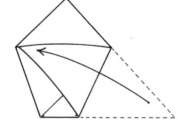

3. Repeat Step 2 with the right point, crossing it over the fold you just made.

4. Now fold the top point down, crease sharply at the rim, then unfold.

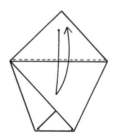

5. Do you see how the flap you folded in Step 3 formed a triangle with a pocket inside? Fold the front flap only of the top point down again—and this time, tuck it into the pocket. It should fit so neatly that it disappears from sight.

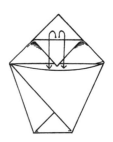

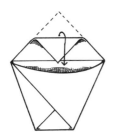

6. Now poke your fingers between the front and back of the form to open up your cup. (Yes, it should be flat at the bottom and rounded at the top.) All that's left to do is fold the remaining top point down and tuck it into the middle of the cup.

CUTE CUP HOLDERS

Want an easy way to organize small items like school supplies or hair accessories? Fold up cups in various colors and sizes, but leave the remaining top point up. Then use pushpins to hang them from their upper flaps on a bulletin board—and fill 'em up!

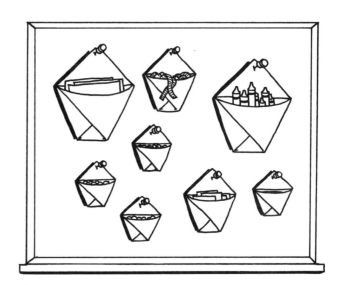

FiRST-TiMER'S TiP!

FOLLOW THE THIN LINE
Always look closely at the thin lines in the illustrations in this book. They show you where your fold is supposed to be. Is the thin line straight up and down? Or is it at an angle? It can make a big difference in the final product. So take your time—and always follow the thin line.

Have a Heart

Let your friends know they're in your heart with a Valentine that you can give any time of year.

MATERIALS

- red or pink origami paper

WHAT TO DO

1. Lay your paper flat in a square, colored side down. Fold it in half from side to side, then unfold it.

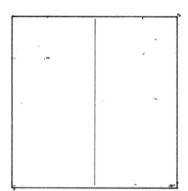

2. Now fold the left and right top corners to the center line.

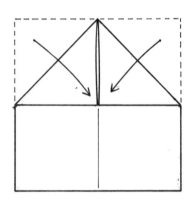

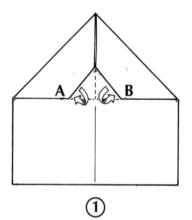

①

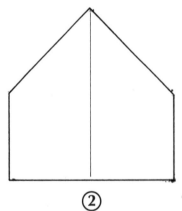

②

3. Use a mountain fold to fold points A and B under, as shown in illustration number 1 on the left. Turn the form over.

4. Fold the left and right sides of the square so they lie flat against the center line.

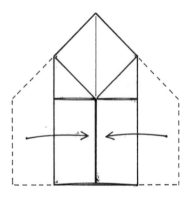

5. Fold the form in half by bringing the top edge down to meet the bottom point. *Voilà!* A heart complete with its own little stand.

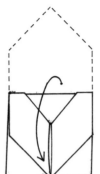

SEND A SECRET NOTE

Share what's in your heart! Write a note on a small piece of paper. Fold it, then slip your note between the folds on the front of the origami heart, which acts as a pocket.

FIRST-TIMER'S TIP!

PRACTICE MAKES PERFECT
If you're folding an origami craft using special paper—like gold foil or an extra-large square—you might want to try making a practice run first using ordinary paper. You won't have to worry about ruining special paper that may be in limited supply.

Whirly Bird

Here's a fun toy that'll keep you and your friends busy—just try not to get dizzy!

MATERIALS

• origami paper

WHAT TO DO

1. Begin with Basic Form 3, open end facing upward.

2. Fold the top point (front flap only) down to meet the bottom point. Turn your form over, and repeat this step on the other side.

3. Now grasp the right point, and fold it over to the left as though you were turning the pages of a book. Turn your form over, and repeat this step on the other side.

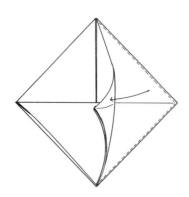

4. Fold the left bottom side (front flap only) so it lies flat against the center line. Repeat this step on the right bottom side.

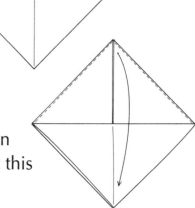

5. Turn your form over, and repeat Step 4 on the other side. Then repeat Step 3 again.

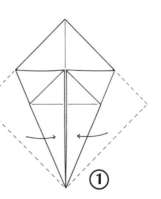

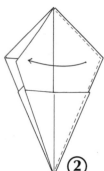

6. Do you see how your form has two points that meet at the top in the middle? Use a valley fold to fold the top left point forward so it sticks straight out from your form. Use a mountain fold to fold the top right point so it points straight back, and your whirly bird is finished.

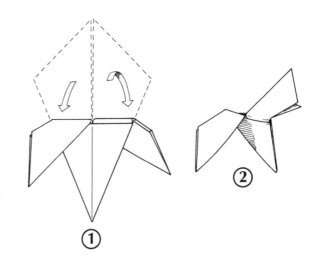

LET IT WHIRL

Stand high up, such as on a chair or at the top of a flight of stairs. Drop the whirly bird, giving it a gentle spin. It will continue whirling all the way to the ground.

FIRST-TIMER'S TIP!

LOOK AHEAD
When you're folding, don't look just at the picture for the step you're on. It helps to look at the next picture as well. That way, you can see not only what fold you're supposed to be doing now, but also what it should look like when it's done.

3-D Tree

Paper is made from trees, so why not make a tree from paper? Follow the steps here, and you'll turn an ordinary piece of paper into a 3-D tree.

MATERIALS

- green origami paper

WHAT TO DO

1. Begin with Basic Form 3, and lay the form so the open ends are facing downward. Fold the left and right top edges (front flaps only) to the center line. Turn your form over, and repeat this step.

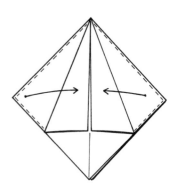

2. Now fold up the front flap of the bottom point. Turn your form over, and repeat this step.

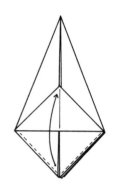

3. Laying the form flat on the table, grasp point A and fold it to the left, as though you were turning a page in a book. Turn your form over and repeat this step.

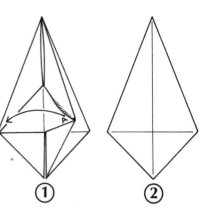

4. Fold the bottom point (front flap only) up and—you guessed it!—turn your form over, and repeat this step.

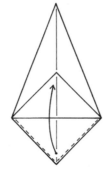

32

5. Slightly separate the front and back sides of the form, and it becomes a 3-D tree.

HOLIDAY HINT

Make this fabulous fir fit for the holidays. Glue on glitter, beads, and a star on top and set it out as a mini–Christmas tree.

FIRST-TIMER'S TIP!

BE A SQUARE

Your paper, that is. When the paper you use to fold your form is perfectly square, you'll find that all your points and edges line up better. To test for squareness, lay your paper flat in a diamond shape and fold it by bringing the top point to meet the bottom. If all your points and your sides are still in line, you've got yourself a square!

Magical Mask

Who's the mystery kid behind that crazy mask? Your friends will want to know—then they'll all want to make a mask of their own.

MATERIALS

- stiff paper, such as construction paper, cut into a 12-inch square
- scissors
- string
- glue
- feathers, buttons, markers, or other decorations

WHAT TO DO

1. Begin with Basic Form 1, and lay it flat. Then fold the top point down so your form has a straight edge across the top.

2. Fold the bottom point up so it touches the center of the top edge.

3. Now fold the bottom point back down so it sticks out below the bottom of your form. This will become a pointed nose.

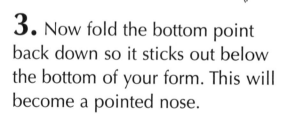

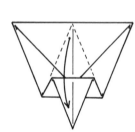

4. Use a mountain fold to fold the form in half by bringing the right side back to meet the left side.

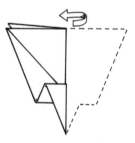

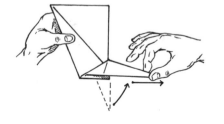

5. Hold your form in one hand while you pull the nose up and to the right. Crease sharply at the back of the nose so it stays firmly in place.

6. You may need an adult's help with this step. Reopen the mask and cut out holes for eyes, then use the points of your scissors to make a hole on each side of the mask near the eyes. Knot a string through each hole so the mask can be placed around your head.

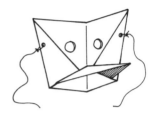

7. Decorate your mask using feathers, buttons, markers, or anything you like—then wear the mask proudly.

THE EYES ARE WATCHING

If you want to display your mask rather than wear it, complete the steps above but stop before you get to Step 6. Then take the point that's slightly hidden behind the nose of your mask, and fold it up so it touches the top edge. Crease it sharply. Then fold it back down so it touches the crease you just made. See how your mask looks like it has eyes? Fold back the left and right sides and the mask will stare at you from a shelf.

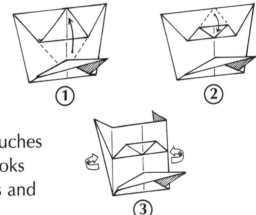

FIRST-TIMER'S TIP!

VALLEYS AND MOUNTAINS
These are two often-used folds. If you tend to forget which fold is which, here's a tip: you run *forward* into a valley, but you climb *back* up the mountain. It's the same way when you fold!

Lady Luckybug

Finding a ladybug is considered good luck, so get a big stack of red paper, and fold some good fortune to pass along to your friends!

MATERIALS

- red origami paper
- black marker

WHAT TO DO

1. Begin with your paper in a diamond shape, white side up. Fold it in half by bringing the top point down to meet the bottom point.

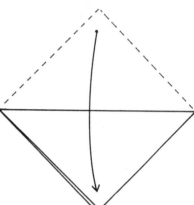

2. Look closely at the illustration for this step. Fold the left and right points down—but instead of folding them so they touch the bottom point, leave a slight gap in between.

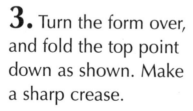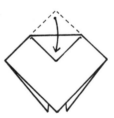

3. Turn the form over, and fold the top point down as shown. Make a sharp crease.

4. To make the ladybug's head, fold the top point back up, making a second crease just below the one you made in Step 3.

5. Turn the form over and you should see the ladybug's head peeking out of its shell.

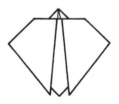

6. Use a mountain fold to fold back the right and left points, as well as the bottom point that's underneath the ladybug's wings.

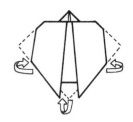

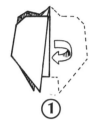 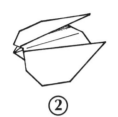
① ②

7. Fold the body in half, using a mountain fold to bring the wings together. Then open the paper until it is not quite flat. This will round out the ladybug's body (because who wants a flattened bug?).

8. Use a black marker to color in the ladybug's head and draw black dots on its body.

WELL WISHES CARD

Have any friends down on their luck? Send some good wishes their way with a card you make yourself! Just fold a sheet of plain, stiff 8½-by-11-inch paper in half, then glue your ladybug on the front. Add a message, like "Ladybugs are for luck, and I feel lucky to have you as a friend!"

FOCUS ON...

MAKING A PLEAT
The ladybug's head is formed by making a pleat—the same kind of pleats you see in skirts or curtains. A pleat is made by stacking one crease above another. The trick is that one crease must be made by using a valley fold, and the other by using a mountain fold. When you push down, one crease will collapse behind the other like an accordion (or a pleat!). Grab a piece of paper and give it a try.

What a Wallet!

Ever wonder why some people call wallets "billfolds"? It's because they're folded—and they hold your bills! Who knew? (Now you do!)

MATERIALS

- 16-inch square of paper (heavy wrapping paper is ideal)
- ruler
- pencil

WHAT TO DO

1. Begin with your paper in a diamond shape, colored side down. Fold it in half by bringing the top point to meet the bottom point.

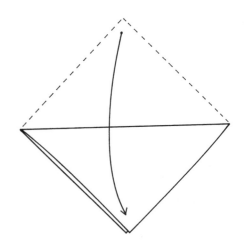

2. Use your ruler to measure along the top edge a third of the way in from the right corner (7½ inches), then make a tiny dot with your pencil.

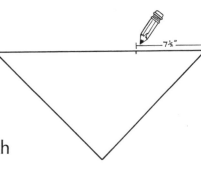

3. Fold the upper left corner over so it just touches the dot. Carefully crease the left vertical edge that you just formed.

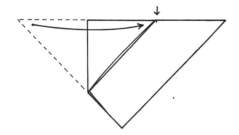

4. Now fold the top right point toward the top left point, and tuck it inside the two sides of the flap you made in Step 3.

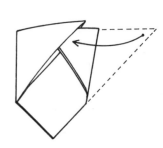

5. Use a valley fold to fold the top edge down, as shown in the illustration.

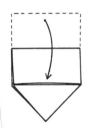

6. Do you see that your form has a top flap that opens like an envelope? Take the bottom point (front flap only) and use a valley fold to fold it up, tucking it between the two layers.

7. Rotate your form so it's pointed-side up. Fold the top forward and down, crease sharply, and your wallet is finished. When you open the wallet, you'll notice that there are two sections for storing money.

 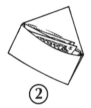

① ②

FUNNY MONEY

If you're giving this wallet as a gift, make play money to put inside. On a piece of paper, trace around a dollar bill. Color it in, then draw a picture in place of George Washington's face, then cut out your funny money.

GET THE POINT
When a form calls for you to line up two points (like Step 1 of this form), you should lay one point carefully on top of the other, then crease at the fold. Now look at the sides of your form. Are they in line, too? If so, great! If not, either your points didn't line up properly or your paper isn't really square. Fix it before you move on to the next step.

Delightful Daffodil

This flower may look just like the real thing, but it will always stay fresh, right down to its curly petals.

MATERIALS

- yellow origami paper
- green pipe cleaner
- toothpick
- scissors

WHAT TO DO

1. Begin with Basic Form 2, and lay it flat so the point faces down.

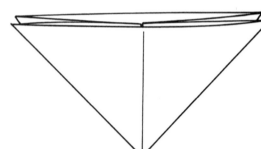

2. Grab hold of the front left side, and fold it so it lies flat against the center line. Crease sharply. Repeat this step on the right side.

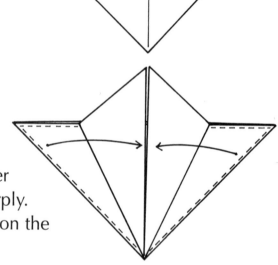

3. Turn your form over and repeat Step 2 on the other side. Your form is now in a kite shape.

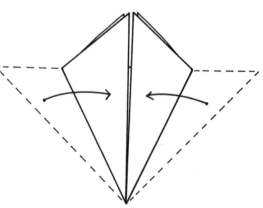

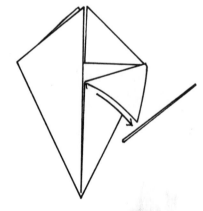

4. See the top right point? That's one of your flower's petals. Give it some curl by rolling it over a toothpick, then sliding the toothpick free. Repeat this step with the other three petals.

5. To make your flower bloom, just poke your fingers inside the middle of the form and spread the petals apart.

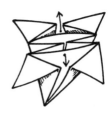

6. Use scissors to snip the bottom tip off your form, then slip a pipe cleaner through the hole. The part that sticks out below your flower is the stem. Allow the pipe cleaner to peek an inch or so above the top of the flower, and curl it around the toothpick to make a stamen.

FRESH-CUT FLOWERS

Grow other flowers from the same form. Do Steps 1 through 3, then use scissors to make a jagged or curved cut across your form like you see here. Tug down the petals. Pretty!

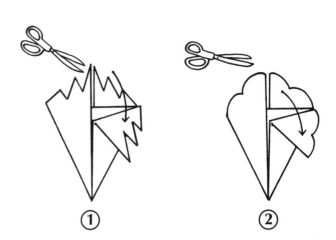

① ②

FiRST-TiMER'S TiP!

MAKE IT LAST
Give your origami crafts long life by spraying them with spray acrylic (ask an adult for help). Another way to add shine and strength is to brush on clear nail polish.

Flutter Bye Butterfly

Choose patterned origami or wrapping paper when you fold your butterfly to give it wildly colored wings.

MATERIALS

- origami paper
- pipe cleaner

WHAT TO DO

1. Start with your paper in a square, colored side down. Fold the paper in half by bringing the bottom edge to meet the top edge, then unfold it. Fold the form in half left to right, then unfold it.

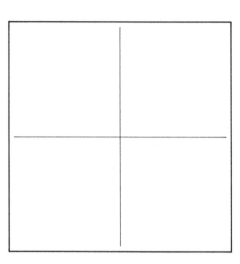

2. Bring each corner in to meet at the center, and fold.

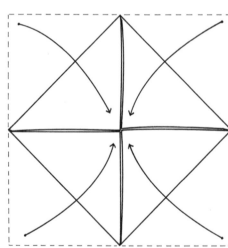

3. Rotate the form so it lies as a square. Fold the form in half with the bottom meeting the top, then unfold. Fold it in half from left to right, then unfold.

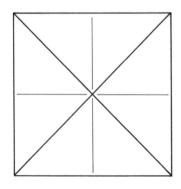

4. Fold the right and left sides to meet at the center line.

5. Fold the top and bottom edges to meet at the center line, then unfold.

6. Make two diagonal creases across the center four squares only. To do this, fold point A to meet point B. Crease the paper sharply, then unfold it. Repeat this step on the opposite side, bringing point C to meet point D, then unfold it.

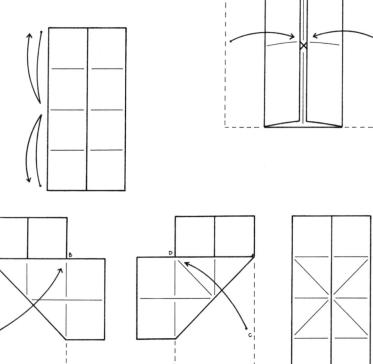

① ② ③

7. This step is a little tricky, so look closely at the illustrations for help. First, grasp the two bottom corners. Then lift them up and gently tug them apart so they flatten and the bottom edge meets the center.

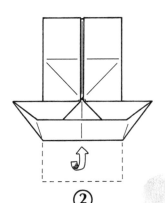

①

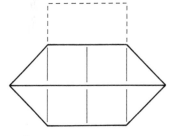

②

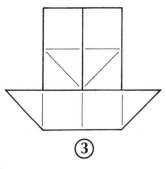

③

8. Repeat Step 7 with the top two corners, pulling them down to meet the center.

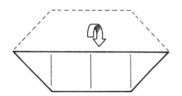

9. Use a mountain fold to fold the form in half, bringing the top to meet the bottom. Your form's open ends should be facing up.

10. Fold the left top point down so the top edge lies against the center line. Repeat this step on the right top point.

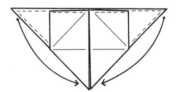

11. Turn your form over. Now just turn back the bottom two points to give each wing more shape.

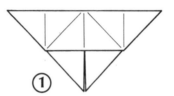 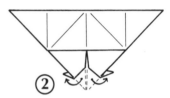

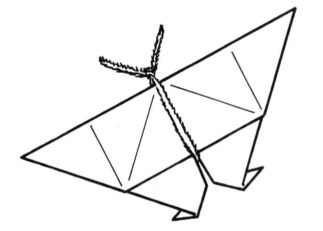

ADD ANTENNAE

Fold a pipe cleaner in half. Wrap it around the spine of your butterfly, then twist the two sides together at the tip and your butterfly is ready to take off.

FiRST-TiMER'S TiP!

FOLDING A POINT TO AN EDGE
When folding a point to an edge of your form, always pay close attention to precisely where the point should rest. Is it right in the middle of the edge? Or is it toward the top or bottom? Getting it just right will make the rest of your folds easier.

Hopping Frog

Want to play leapfrog? All you need is a piece of green paper and a few minutes to fold up a frog so cute it'll jump right into your heart!

MATERIALS

- green origami paper
- black marker and dark green or brown marker

WHAT TO DO

1. Begin with your paper flat in a square, colored side down. Fold it in half by bringing the top edge to meet the bottom edge, then fold it in half again by folding the left edge to meet the right edge. Reopen it into a square.

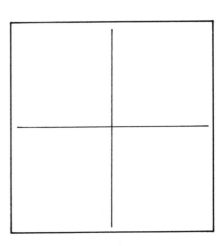

2. Fold each of the four corners to the center point of your form.

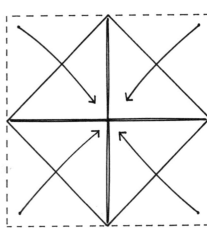

3. Fold the left and right upper edges in so they lie flat against the center line.

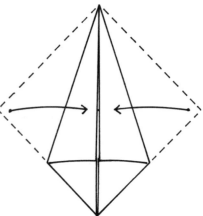

4. Fold the bottom point up to the center of the form, creasing it at the base.

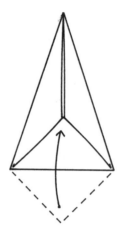

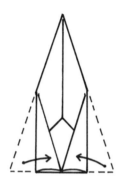

5. Now fold the bottom left point to the center line at the base of your form. Crease it firmly, then repeat this step on the bottom right point. If your form looks like a house with a narrow pointed roof, you're "hopping" right along!

6. Bring the bottom edge up so it just touches the bottom of the "roof," then fold it halfway back down.

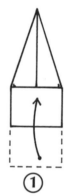

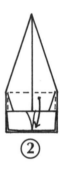

① ②

7. Fold the top point about a third of the way down the form, then flip the form over.

8. Draw two dots for eyes, and decorate the frog's back with dark spots.

46

HOW TO DO THE HOP

To make your leapin' frog leap, press down with your finger at the back fold. When you slide your finger back, watch that froggie go! Try making two frogs, and challenge a friend to a good old-fashioned frog race.

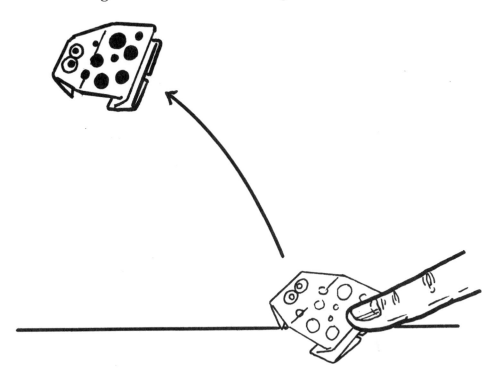

FIRST-TIMER'S TIP!

PUT IT TO USE

Tell your origami crafts, "Don't just sit there!" Instead, put them to work! A metal pin fastener can make your paper art into a pin you can wear. Or glue a magnet to the back of a form and stick it on your refrigerator. Crafts like this frog also make great gift toppers, holiday ornaments, or cards. Can you think of new ways to put your paper projects to use?

Ship Shape

This ship is actually seaworthy for a minute or two—but if you're folding it for keeps, you'll want to limit your sailing adventures to somewhere dry, like a tabletop.

MATERIALS

- origami paper

WHAT TO DO

1. Begin with your paper flat in a diamond shape, colored side up. Fold it in half by bringing the left point to meet the right.

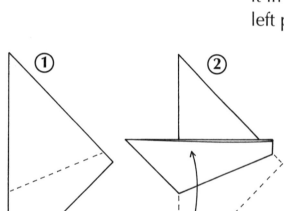

2. Take a look at the dotted line shown here. Use a valley fold to bring the bottom edge up so it is straight across, creasing it at the dotted line. (For an extra-sharp crease, try the First-Timer's Tip on page 15.) This step gives you a glimpse of the shape your ship is going to take—but it's not done yet!

3. Unfold your form so it is again flat in a diamond shape. Do you see how the crease on the right side of your form bends in a different direction than the one on the left? You're going to change that! Use a mountain fold to bring the top and bottom right edges toward each other in the back, then pinch along the crease. Unfold the form again.

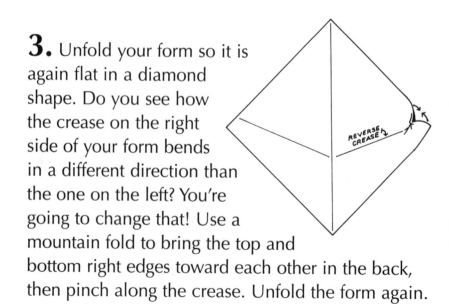

REVERSE CREASE

48

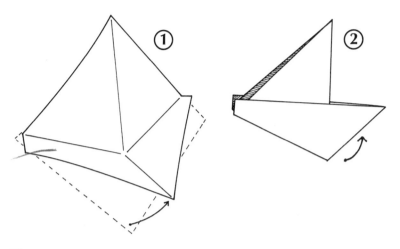

① ②

4. Turn the form over. Lift the bottom edges up, which will make the bottom point stick straight out.

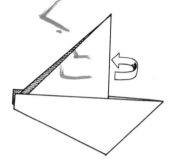

5. Now use a mountain fold to bring the bottom right point to meet the left. Flatten all creases well, and you have a colorful ship with a white sail.

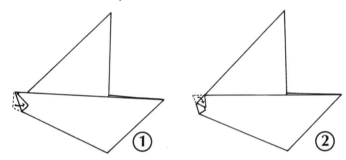

① ②

6. All that's left to do is fold the bottom left front and back corners as seen in the illustrations.

AND THEY'RE OFF!

Place your ship at the edge of a table or on the floor, then send it sailing by blowing on the back opening of the sails. Fold up more than one ship, and have a day at the races.

FiRST-TiMER'S TiP!

TAKE IT ONE STEP AT A TIME
For the best results, always do every step and in the order shown. It may be tempting to skip ahead, but that may confuse you later.

Pecking Crow

Here is origami in action! Make a hungry crow that pecks at the ground no matter how many times you try to set him straight.

MATERIALS

- black origami paper
- orange paint
- paintbrush
- two googly eyes (available at arts and crafts stores)
- glue

WHAT TO DO

1. Begin with Basic Form 1, then turn it on its side with the long point facing left. Fold the form in half by bringing the top point to meet the bottom.

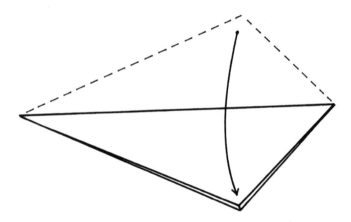

2. Look closely at the illustrations for this step. Use a valley fold to fold the left point over at the diagonal shown. Crease it sharply, then unfold it.

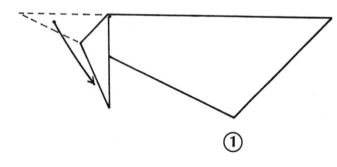

①

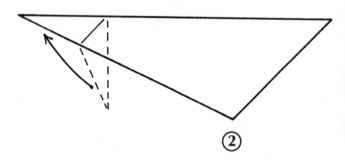

②

3. Your crow can't peck without a beak! To give him one, you'll need to do an inside-reverse fold. Ready? Start by pinching the middle of the form together at the top with your right hand. With your other hand, slightly separate the front and back flaps of the form, then push the left point in between them so it bends at the crease and points down at an angle. When you do this, it will actually turn that piece inside out and make the crow's pointy beak.

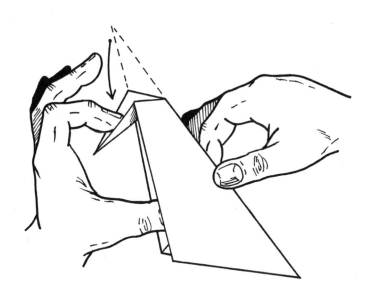

4. Paint the beak orange, and glue on two googly eyes. Then go ahead and try to stand the crow on his base. He'll automatically tip over to "peck" at the ground!

DID YOU KNOW?

Traditionally, most origami crafts were models of birds, fish, and plants. That's because origami is more than a thousand years old, and life in Japan and China (where origami is said to have started) centered around the sea, the sky, and the earth.

FIRST-TIMER'S TIP!

THE INSIDE-REVERSE FOLD

This form uses an inside-reverse fold (in Step 3), which is one of the trickier folds to learn—but one that will allow you to do more advanced origami crafts. The secret to getting it right is remembering the name: inside-reverse. That's because whatever point you're folding is going to wind up inside your form, and it will reverse and turn inside out. Now that you know what you're supposed to do, grab some paper and go for it!

Great Gift Box

It's said that good things come in small packages. When you give a gift in a box you've made yourself, the package is every bit as special as what's inside!

MATERIALS

- origami paper

WHAT TO DO

1. Begin with your paper in a square, colored side down. Make a crease along the center by folding the top to meet the bottom, then unfolding.

2. Fold the top and bottom edges to the center line.

3. Fold all four corners so they touch the center line. This means that you'll fold the top corners downward and the bottom corners upward.

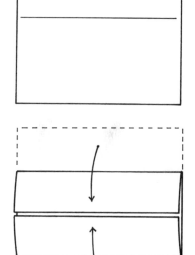

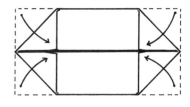

4. Take the left point and fold it over to the center crease, crease it as shown in the illustration, then unfold. Repeat this step with the right point.

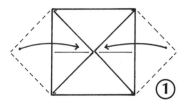

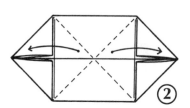

5. Open the upper left corner to form a square. Then fold the top flap only up and across as shown. Fold the corner so it touches the center line again. Repeat this step with the other three corners.

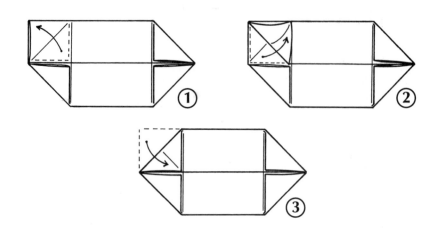

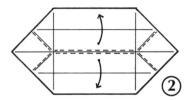

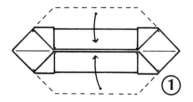

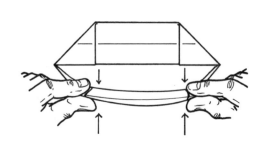

6. Turn the form over. Fold the top and bottom edges to the center line, then unfold.

7. Turn the form over. Ready? Put your index fingers just below the center opening of the form. Put your thumbs near the bottom, below the crease. Now pinch just the top layer of paper together, sliding your index fingers toward your thumbs. This will form one side of your box.

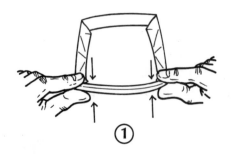

8. Turn your form so the top is now the bottom, and repeat Step 7. When you do this, the other sides of the box will automatically be drawn up. Simply tuck the sides of the box into place, and your box is complete.

TO MAKE A LID

Choose paper about 1 inch larger in size than what you used to fold the box, then fold it following Steps 1 through 8. Your lid will fit neatly on top. If you want, tear apart several cotton balls to line your box with soft cotton.

A TREASURE BOX

Brighten up a plain box by adding plastic gems, buttons, and beads. You can glue them on the lid of your box, or add more pizzazz by outlining the area with a dab of puff paint, then placing the jewels on top. The paints will hold the treasures in place as well as add some color around the edges.

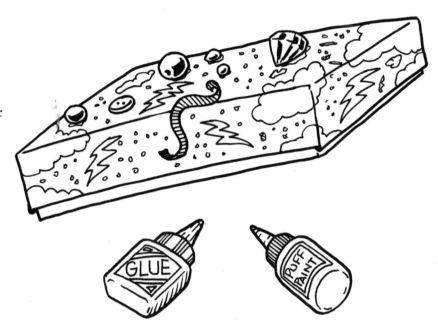

The Amazing Climbing Monkey

You'll laugh out loud as you watch this little paper monkey climb up inside the mountain, then pop out the top!

MATERIALS

- origami paper
- scissors

WHAT TO DO

1. Begin with Basic Form 3, and lay it so the open ends are facing downward.

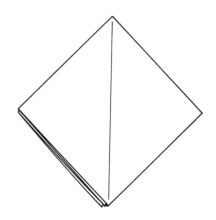

2. Using your scissors, snip the very tip of the form off to form a tiny triangle. This is your monkey. Save this piece—you will need it later.

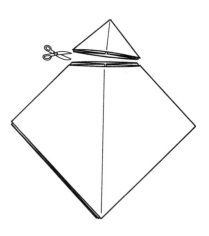

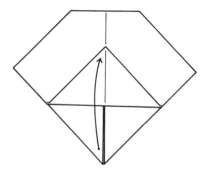

3. Fold the bottom point (front flap only) up so it's just below the top edge.

4. Turn your form over, and repeat this step on the other side.

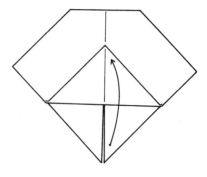

5. Now you're ready to let your monkey climb the mountain. To do this, pull the bottom points of the mountain slightly apart from each other. Then thread the tiny triangle piece between these points. Each bottom point should fit between the front and back flaps of the triangle.

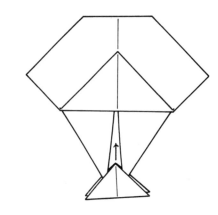

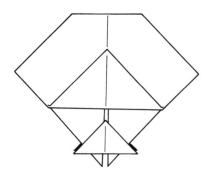

6. Slide the monkey up so it's at the base of the mountain.

7. To make the monkey start climbing, hold the form in your hands and move the bottom points up and down, as if you were milking a cow. The only difference is that instead of going straight up and down, let the points slightly overlap as you move them. Amazingly, your monkey will climb the mountain, and leap out the top.

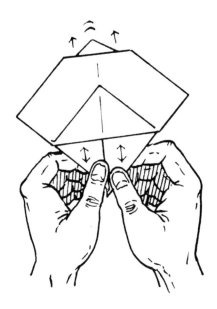

MAKE IT MAGIC

Show your friends how you make the monkey climb, then challenge them to give it a try. Chances are, they won't have noticed how you made the bottom points overlap as you moved them up and down. Tell them that only *you* know the secret of the mountain—that is, until you're ready to share it!

DID YOU KNOW?

This game is sometimes also called "Climbing Mount Fuji," after one of the most well-known mountains in Japan. Check an atlas and see if you can locate this world-famous mountain.

Cottage, Sweet Cottage

No big, bad wolf would ever want to blow down a cottage this cute. Forget the bricks—your home of paper is sturdy enough to stand its ground.

MATERIALS

- origami paper
- markers

WHAT TO DO

1. Begin with a square piece of paper. Fold it in half from side to side. Reopen the paper to a flat square, then fold it in half from top to bottom. Reopen the paper.

2. Fold the top edge down to the center line. Turn the form over.

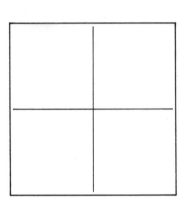

3. Use a valley fold to bring the left and right sides to the center line.

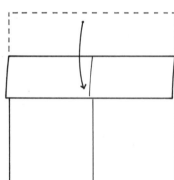

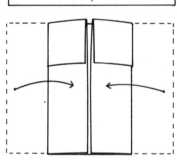

4. Get ready to raise the roof, which you'll do by using a squash fold. Start by finding the little square flaps at the top of your form. Then poke your finger into the left flap. Pull point A to the left while you squash point B to make a triangle shape. That's it!

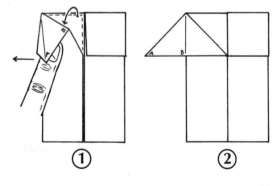

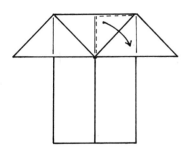

5. Repeat Step 4 on the right flap.

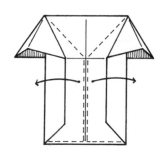

6. The sides of your house meet at the center line of your form. Pull them out so they stand straight up from the form. Turn your form over and stand your house up.

7. Use markers to draw windows, a door, and other details.

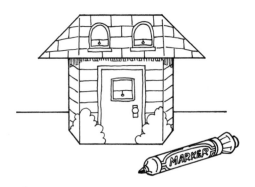

YOUR DREAM HOUSE

Amaze your family by creating a house that looks just like your own, or your grandparents'—or even a favorite house near where you live. Start with paper that matches the outside of your dream house. After you've folded it, use markers and cut paper to add details like roof tiles, shutters, and doors.

FOCUS ON...

SQUASH FOLD
To make the cottage, you'll need to do a squash fold in Steps 4 and 5. It's called a squash fold because that's exactly what you do: you take part of your origami fold (usually a flap) and use your fingers to squash it flat. It may take a try or two to get the hang of it, but once you do, you'll be a squashing maniac!

Fox Finger Puppet

It's showtime! With its pointed ears and rounded face, this fox puppet will be the hit of any play.

MATERIALS

- origami paper
- googly eyes (available at arts and crafts stores)
- glue

WHAT TO DO

1. Begin with your paper in a square, then fold it in half from side to side. Reopen it.

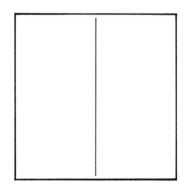

2. Fold your form in half by bringing the top edge to meet the bottom edge.

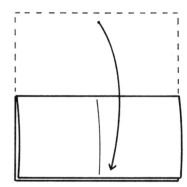

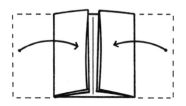

3. Fold the left and right sides to meet at the center line.

4. Use a valley fold to fold point A down so it touches the left side. Unfold. Now fold point B down to the right side. Unfold.

①

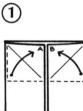

②

5. Now lift the right front flap so it sticks straight up from your form. Poke your finger in between the sides of the flap, then push on the point to squash it flat. It should look like a triangle sitting on top of a rectangle, as shown here.

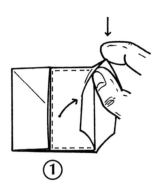

① ②

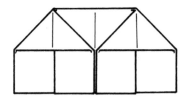

6. Repeat Step 5 on the left front flap.

7. Use mountain folds to fold the right and left sides of your form so they meet the back center line.

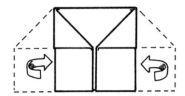

8. Fold up the lower left point (front flap only) to a little above the center of your form as shown. Turn your form over.

9. Fold up the lower right point to a little above the center of your form as shown.

10. Turn your form so it's upside down. It should look like a house with a roof that's slanted on one side and straight across on the other side.

11. Take the top point (front flap only) and fold it down so the left diagonal edge lies flat against the center horizontal line. Turn your form over.

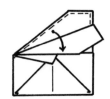

12. Now fold the top point down so the right diagonal edge meets the center line.

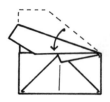

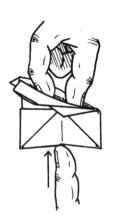

13. Ready to turn your flat form into a fat fox? Slip your fingers between the front and back sides at the top of your form. Pull them apart, and at the same time, push in on the center of the bottom edge. What you're actually doing is pushing the fox's ears apart, and pushing in to form its mouth.

14. Glue on googly eyes, and slip your thumb and finger in the back to make your fox puppet start talking.

PUPPET PALS

Fold up some friends for your fox by making masks (see directions on page 34) using 8-inch squares of paper. Glue each mask to the top of a Popsicle stick, and you'll have plenty of puppets to put on a show-stopping performance.

FIRST-TIMER'S TIP!

GIVE IT A FINISHING TOUCH
Your origami crafts will look more polished if you take a moment after you're done folding to pinch and crease all the edges again so they're neatly in place.

A Tisket . . . a Tiny Basket

Have a pal who's feeling down? Share some cheer by bringing a basket "special delivery" filled with tiny treats.

MATERIALS

- 6-inch square of origami paper
- pencil
- ruler
- raffia or ribbon
- scissors
- stapler

WHAT TO DO

1. Begin with your paper flat in a diamond shape, colored side down. Fold it in half by bringing the top point to meet the bottom point. Open it.

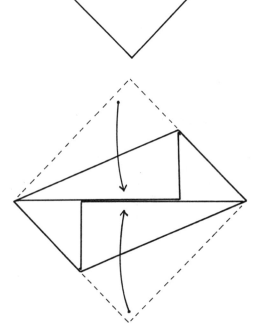

2. Fold the top point and its left edge to the center line. Take the bottom point and its right edge, and fold it to the center line.

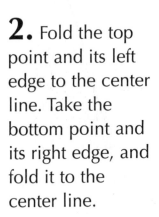

3. Take the new bottom point and its left edge, and fold it to the center. Then take the top point and right edge, and fold it to the center.

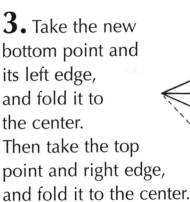

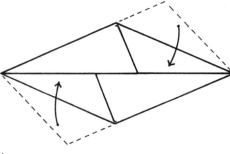

4. You now have a diamond shape. Fold it in half by bringing the top point over to meet the bottom.

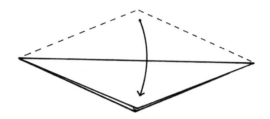

5. Use your ruler to measure 2 inches in from the left end, and make a tiny dot with your pencil. Repeat this step on the right side.

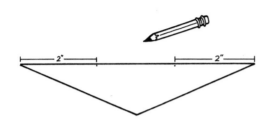

6. Use a valley fold to bring the points on the left and right sides down, bending them at the spot you just marked at a slight diagonal, as shown in the illustration. Crease well, then unfold them.

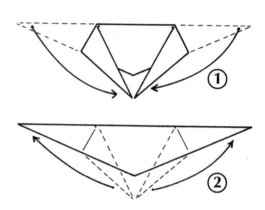

7. Ready to make the handles of your basket? Start on the right side, and use an inside-reverse fold to poke this part of the form inside, as shown in the illustration. The easiest way to do this is to push in and down on the top edge just to the right of your pencil mark.

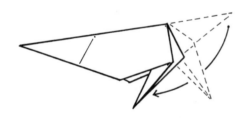

8. Repeat Step 7 on the left side of your form.

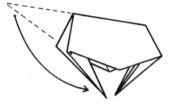

9. Turn your form upside down and your basket is nearly ready! Cut a few strips of raffia or ribbon, and tie them into a bow. Place the bow at the handle tip. Ask an adult to help you use a stapler to secure the bow and the two handle points together.

THINK BIG

A 18-inch square of paper
will give you a basket
large enough to hold rolls
or crackers on your dining
room table. (In Step 5,
you'll need to measure
6 inches in on each side,
instead of 2 inches.)

MEASURING UP
Sometimes you can "eyeball it" when you're making a fold, which means
guessing where you should fold based on what looks right. To be
precise, however, it helps to pull out your ruler and measure if you
need to make a crease in an exact spot.

A Perfect Penguin

Use paper that's black on one side and white on the other to give your penguin its proper tuxedo attire.

MATERIALS

- origami paper (black on one side, white on the other)
- white crayon

WHAT TO DO

1. Start with your paper in a diamond shape, black side up. Fold the bottom point up about a third of the way.

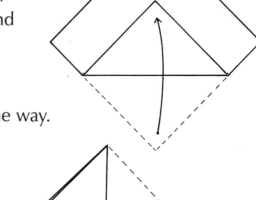

2. Now fold the form in half by bringing the right side over to the left.

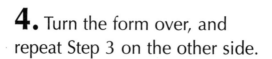

3. Use a valley fold to fold the left point (front flap only) until it just touches the right side—this will be the penguin's flipper.

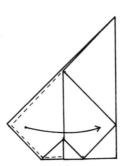

4. Turn the form over, and repeat Step 3 on the other side.

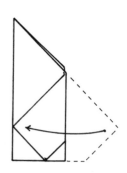

5. Fold down the top point about 1½ inches from the tip at a slight diagonal as shown. Make a sharp crease, then unfold it.

6. To create a head, first slightly reopen the form. Pull down on the top point, allowing the form to bend along the crease you just created in Step 5. Continue pushing the top point toward the center until the form automatically closes back up.

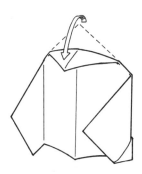

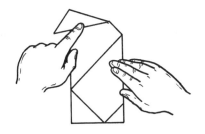

7. Lay the form down, and flatten all folds.

8. Use a white crayon to draw on eyes, and admire your perfect penguin in its "tux and tails."

BE AN INDIVIDUAL

Why not try folding several penguins, experimenting with giving them different-sized heads and wings. Take a look at Steps 1 and 5 in this form—what your penguin looks like will depend on exactly where you fold your points and make your creases.

FIRST-TIMER'S TIP!

MAKE YOUR OWN TWO-SIDED PAPER
If you don't have origami paper that's black on one side and white on the other, you can make your own. Just cut two same-sized squares of paper, a black one and a white one. Then glue them back to back.

Two-Part Paper Puppy

You'll need two pieces of paper to fold this clever puppy that even knows a trick—it stands up on its own.

MATERIALS

- two squares of paper, each the same size
- colored pencils

WHAT TO DO

1. This is a two-part form, and you'll start by making the puppy's head. Lay one of your pieces of paper flat in a diamond shape, colored side down. Fold it in half by bringing the top point to meet the bottom point.

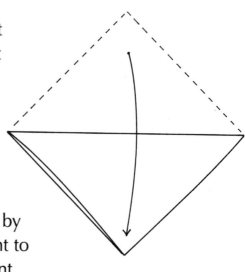

2. To give your puppy floppy ears, fold the left and right points down at an angle like you see here.

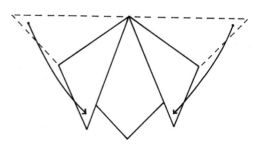

3. Now use a mountain fold to fold both the top and bottom points back as shown. Make sure the front bottom flap is folded so it is inside the form, while the back bottom flap is behind the form.

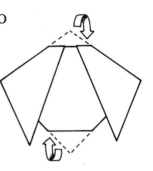

4. Draw on eyes, a nose, and a mouth, and you're ready for the next step.

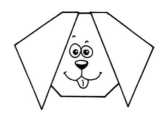

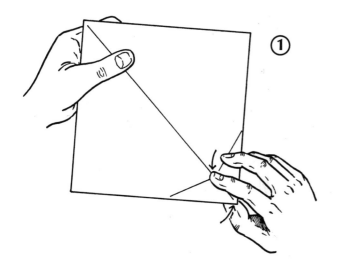

5. Take your other piece of paper and lay it flat in a square, colored side down. Make it into a triangle by folding the upper right corner down to meet the lower left corner.

6. Use a valley fold to bring the lower point up as shown. Crease sharply, then unfold it. Now use a mountain fold at that same crease, then unfold it. (Creasing the paper in both directions will make the outside-reverse fold in the next step easier to do.)

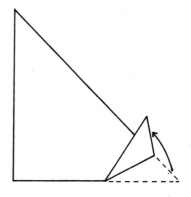

7. Now you're going to use an outside-reverse fold to turn the little flap you just made into a perky tail. Open the sides of your form so it's nearly unfolded. Then, holding the form with your left hand, push down on the exact spot where your creases meet in an X while you push up on the lower right point. This will make the tail turn inside out. Reclose your form and sharpen all creases.

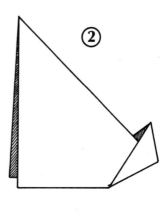

①   ②

8. Set the puppy's head on top of its body by slipping the top point of the body between the bottom flaps of the head. Stand your origami friend where everyone can see him.

IT'S A CAT-ASTROPHE

Make a cat's head instead of a dog's by using a square of paper and following Steps 1, 2, and 3. Now fold up the ears as shown. Draw on eyes, a nose, and whiskers.

FIRST-TIMER'S TIP!

OUTSIDE-REVERSE FOLD
**The tail of your pup is folded using an outside-reverse fold (see Step 7).
It's easier than you might think, as long as you do exactly what it sounds
like you should do: fold a point so that it stays outside the form, but
reverses to flip inside out.**

Floatable Boat

Fold, fold, fold your boat, gently down the stream—or at least across your bathtub. This rowboat really floats when you set it in water.

MATERIALS

• origami paper

WHAT TO DO

1. Begin with your paper flat in a square, colored side up. Fold it in half by bringing the top edge to meet the bottom edge, then unfold.

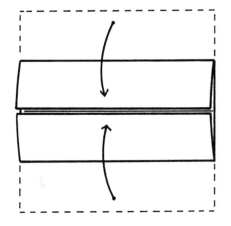

2. Now fold the top and bottom edges to meet at the center line.

3. Fold all four corners so they touch the center line. This means that you'll fold the top corners downward and the bottom corners upward.

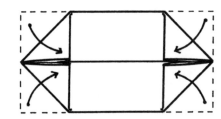

4. Now fold the upper left point (point A) to the center line, creasing at a diagonal, as shown in the illustration. Repeat this step on points B, C, and D.

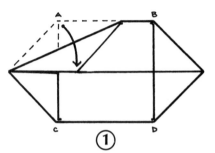 ①

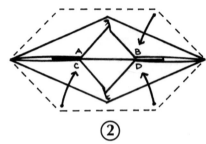 ②

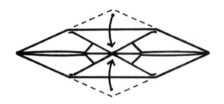

5. Use a valley fold to fold the top and bottom points to the center line. Crease all your edges firmly.

6. To make your boat ready to float, you have to actually flip the form inside out! (If this sounds hard, imagine you're trying to turn a hat inside out—could you do that? This is similar.) The first thing you need to do is pull apart the top and bottom edges at the center line. Do you see the colored part of your paper inside? This will soon be the outside of your rowboat.

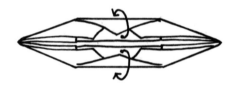

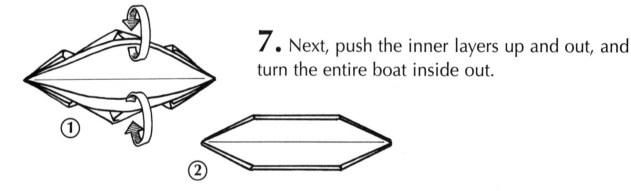

7. Next, push the inner layers up and out, and turn the entire boat inside out.

8. Turn your boat over. Use your fingers to round out the bottom of your rowboat and to pinch points on the bow and stern (that's the front and back for you landlubbers). Your boat is ready to sail.

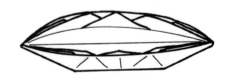

HAPPY SAILS TO YOU

Your boat will float better if you weigh it down a bit, which you can do by adding sails. Just take a dime-sized circle of clay, and set it in the bottom of your boat. Then press a wooden toothpick into the clay. Cut square-shaped sails out of tissue paper, and thread them onto the toothpick.

FIRST-TIMER'S TIP!

FIXING MISTAKES

What do you do if you get to a step, and you find your form no longer matches the illustration? Let's say, for example, the instructions say to lift the flap, and you don't have a flap. The first thing you should do is unfold the form back to a step where you were sure everything was in the right place. Then check carefully as you move ahead from there, taking the time to read the instructions and look at the illustrations as you go. Usually, it's something simple that you missed, and you'll be back on track in no time. (And if you really can't undo the damage, get a new square of paper and start over.)

The Peace Crane

The crane, a sacred bird, is the traditional symbol of peace in Japan.

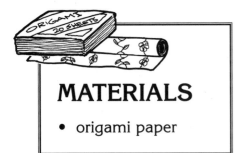

MATERIALS

• origami paper

WHAT TO DO

1. Begin with Basic Form 3, and lay it so the open ends are facing down.

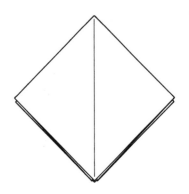

2. Using only the top layer of paper, fold points A and B to the center line.

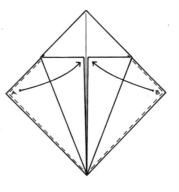

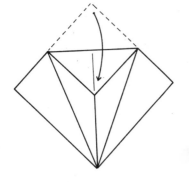

3. Now fold down the top point, creasing it firmly across the top.

4. Unfold the form back to a small diamond.

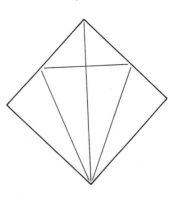

5. This step is a little tough, but don't get discouraged. First, lift up the bottom point (top layer only) and pull it toward the top of the form, flattening the flap into a long diamond shape.

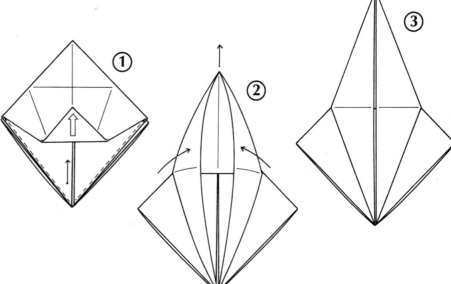

6. Turn the form over, and repeat Steps 2 through 5.

7. Lay the form flat so the end that has an opening between the two sides is pointing down.

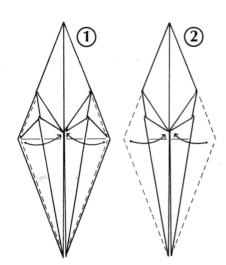

8. Fold the left and right points (top layer only) toward the center line so the bottom edges lie flat against the center line. Turn your form over and repeat this step on the other side.

9. Make a diagonal crease on the bottom right flap of the form, as shown in the illustration. Then unfold it.

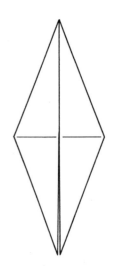

10. To make the crane's neck, lift point A up, separating the two sides of the piece. This part of the form will now turn inside out.

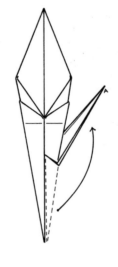

11. Grasp the neck about one third of the way down from the tip. Gently pull point A down. While you do this, the neck will automatically open up and will tuck inside the head. Stop moving point A once the head is in position, and flatten all folds.

12. The top two points are the wings. Pull them out and away from each other until the crane's body fills out.

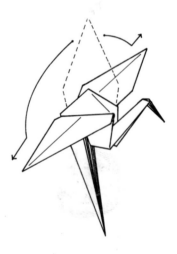

DID YOU KNOW?

The crane is a sacred bird in Japan. According to legend, it may live for a thousand years. A person who folds a thousand cranes, making the same wish with each one, will have her wish granted.

Hot-Air Balloon

Pucker up and blow to watch this amazing origami balloon inflate right before your eyes!

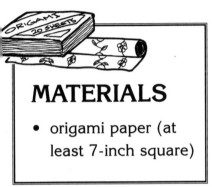

MATERIALS

- origami paper (at least 7-inch square)

WHAT TO DO

1. Begin with Basic Form 2.

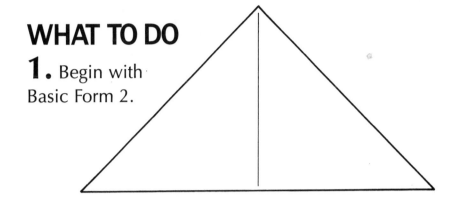

2. Fold the lower left and right corners (front flaps only) to the top point. Turn your form over, and repeat this step.

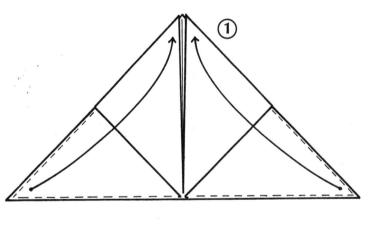

①

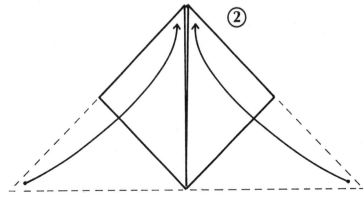

②

3. Now fold the front flaps so the right and left side points touch the center line. Turn the form over again and repeat this step on the other side.

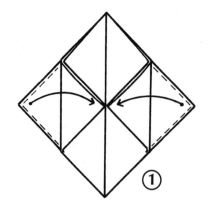

①

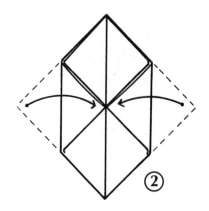

②

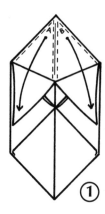

①

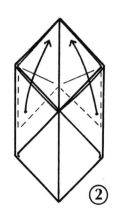

②

4. Fold points A and B down (front flaps only). Make sharp creases, then unfold.

5. Next, tuck points A and B into the center triangles, as shown in the illustration. To do this, open the triangle pockets with your fingers and slip the edges in. You'll be able to see a tiny bit of them still sticking out of the pockets—that's okay!

6. Turn your form over and repeat Steps 4 and 5 on the other side.

7. It's time to inflate your balloon. Find the tiny hole at the bottom of your form. Then blow into it, and your form will fill with air.

TUCKING A POINT

It can sometimes be difficult to tuck a point into a pocket (like you do in Step 5), but there are ways to make it easier. One trick is to poke the pocket open first with your fingers before inserting the point. Another is to fold the point over the top of the pocket first, crease it, then poke it inside.

Love origami? You're not the only one! Here are a few places you can learn more about origami and connect with others who are interested in the art of folding paper.

ORIGAMI USA

This national origami organization gives news on events and exhibits, and tips on making great origami crafts. When you visit Origami USA's Web site, you can also contact an origami volunteer who will answer your questions about paper folding.
15 West 77 St.
New York, NY 10024-5192
Phone: (212) 769-5635
Web site: **www.origami-usa.org**

JOSEPH WU'S ORIGAMI PAGE

There are lots of origami sites on the Internet. (With your parent's help, you can do a search under the term *origami*. You'll be amazed!) Joseph Wu's Origami Page is one of the most popular. You'll find it at **www.origami.vancouver.bc.ca**. It features sample crafts, news on origami, tips for success, and more.

SUPPORT THE ARTS...AND KIDS!

You can buy handcrafted origami stars and other crafts at **www.1000cranes.com**. Profits from sales benefit children's hospitals and cancer research.

MORE BOOKS

Once you've mastered the crafts here, check out these other origami books published by Lowell House:

50 Nifty Super Animal Origami Crafts
50 Nifty Super Origami Crafts
Girls Wanna Have Fun: Friendship Origami
Holiday Origami (updated edition)
Super Nifty Origami Crafts